Noah and His Ark

Retold by Catherine Storr

Pictures by Jim Russell

Methuen Children's Books
in association with Belitha Press Ltd

Once upon a time there lived a man called Noah.
He had a wife, Mrs Noah.
And three sons, Shem, Ham and Japheth.
The sons had wives too,
Mrs Shem, Mrs Ham and Mrs Japheth.

One day, Noah heard God say to him,
'Noah! There is going to be a great flood,
and everyone in the world will be drowned.
You'll be the only people left alive.

You must start at once to build a huge ship,
with windows and doors. It must be big enough
to hold you and your family and
two of every kind of animal you can find.'

Noah called his three sons,
Shem, Ham and Japheth,
and they went up the mountainside
and cut down trees and sawed them into planks.
They began to build the huge ship.
They called it the Ark.

Noah's neighbours came and laughed at him.
'What a stupid thing to do!' they said.
'Why build a huge great ship like this,
miles away from the sea?'
'Because there is going to be a great flood,'
Noah told them,
but this only made them laugh still more.

At last the Ark was finished. Noah and his sons
and their wives went off to collect the animals.
They found elephants, bears, zebras,
cats, rabbits, mice, even spiders and ants.

Two of every kind came into the Ark,
and were shown the stables,
the cages and the rooms where they were to live.
The Ark was very crowded.

Just as the last tiny creature got inside,
the rain began.
At first Noah's neighbours went on laughing.
'Just a shower!' they said.
But as the rain went on and the rivers rose
and the sea began to swell, they were frightened.

First the water covered the roads
and the fields.
Then it came up to the windows of the houses.
Then it came up to the roofs of the houses
and the tops of the trees.

At last there was nothing
to be seen in the whole world,
but the Ark, sailing all alone
in the world of water.
And still it went on raining.

Noah told his family what to do.
'Shem, you and your wife must feed all the animals.
We have plenty of leaves and corn for the elephants
and the rabbits. Ask the cow to give you milk
for the cats. Don't let them eat the mice.
Tell the bees to make honey for the bears.'

'Ham,' Noah said, 'You and Mrs Ham must keep
the animals clean.
Sweep out the stables and wash the cages.
Put all the dung into the special hole we made for it.
We shall need it when the rain stops
and we have to plant seeds in the earth.'

'Japheth, you and Mrs Japheth must collect
the rain water as it falls on the Ark,
so that we have fresh water to drink
and to wash with.

Mrs Noah is going to cook for all of us,
and I will help everyone at their work.'
'Not me,' said Mrs Noah.
'I like to have my kitchen to myself.'

After forty long days and nights, the rain stopped.
There was no dry land to be seen.
Noah sent off a raven to look for land.
It did not come back, so Noah sent out a dove.
But the dove could not find any land,
and she came back to the Ark to rest.

A week later, Noah sent the dove out again,
and that evening she came back with a leaf
from an olive tree in her beak.
Then Noah knew that the waters were sinking,
and soon they would see dry land again.

After another seven days,
Noah sent the dove out again.
This time she did not come back at all,
so he knew she had found
some land where she could build her nest.
Soon afterwards the Ark came to rest on dry land.

Noah opened the door of the Ark
and all the animals were very glad to come out.
Noah said to them, 'Go off, stretch your legs,
eat all you can find and have lots of babies
to fill this empty world.'
Noah and his family were glad
to get out of the Ark. They began
to build houses and to make gardens
and to work in the fields again.

They wondered at first if there might be another flood,
but God promised that this would never happen again.
To show that he remembered his promise,
God put a rainbow in the sky.

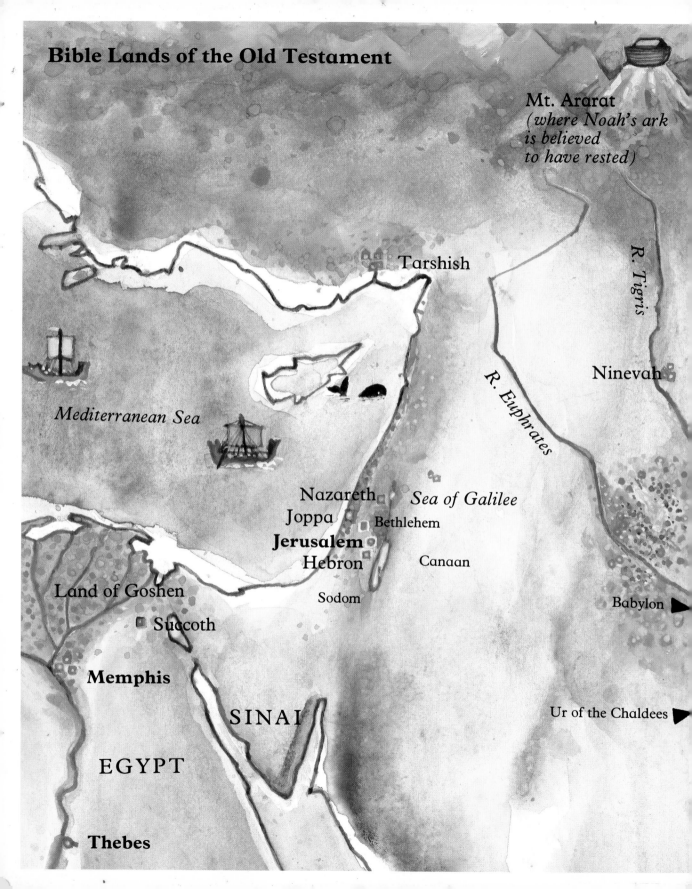